Hechizo

Poems

Mark Statman

Lavender Ink
New Orleans

Hechizo
Mark Statman

Printed in the U.S.A.
First Printing
10 9 8 7 6 5 4 3 2 1   19 20 21 22 23 24

Book design: Bill Lavender.
Cover Photo: Katherine Koch
Cover art: *Alebrije* mask by Oscar Carillo and Josefina
Morales, collection Katherine Koch and Mark Statman

Library of Congress Control Number: 2021948571
Statman, Mark
Hechizo / Mark Statman;
p. cm.
ISBN: 978-1-944884-96-3 (pbk.)

Lavender Ink
lavenderink.org

Also by Mark Statman

The Red Skyline (poems)
*Listener in the Snow: The Practice and Teaching of
   Poetry*
*The Alphabet of the Trees: A Guide to Nature
   Writing* (co-edited with Christian McEwen)
Poet in New York, Federico García Lorca
   (translated with Pablo Medina)
Tourist at a Miracle (poems)
*Black Tulips: The Selected Poems of José María
   Hinojosa* (translation)
A Map of the Winds (poems)
That Train Again (poems)
*Never Made in America: Selected Poems from
   Martín Barea Mattos* (translation)
Exile Home (poems)

Contents

IV. *Hechizo* (love poems)

Hechizo

I. The Furies (*duende*)

the furies argue

are you
wrestling with
sanity are
you at the
edge are you
staring too
hard at the
sky at
stars the stars
the beating
fury wings a
whisper
promise they
claim perfection
and the world
gesturing at
dreams so
beatific their
counsel
annihilate yourself
dissolve fall
into their arms
take their love
ever more deeply
to your heart

kabbala

turn off the light for

the mountain in the
distance a sign points
in the other direction saying
the path is over
there the other
way the prayer
says ask the stranger
in the road ask the beggar
among you with his hourglass
his outstretched hand
with words written on his
face and you
                    walk the
distance into the nowhere
it's that long it's that slow
the night you turn the
light back on trace the
letters in the book master
the words master the
language say to yourself
there's no matter there's
no substance the soul
calls out *here I am*
far from the
mountains far from the river
far the cities and crowds
the deserts the forests
it's so far from anywhere
there's anyone

                    your soul innocent

your body isn't those
ruins of your own making ruins
of spinning selves
measured against another
prayer a psalm the
hearts of the angels so close their
hearts and your heart beating
you feel it hard and frightening
one breath another breath one
after another the mysterious
closing in on you the
mysterious world the
mysterious worlds you
imagine a fire that might
warm you now the nights
have been colder
cold endless or
infinite it's hard to know
which hard to know
why the pointing
signs had not been inscribed
more simply *go back*

lizard

off in the sunset the
sinuous savior road the
path the trail what's
around the turn the
lizard lizard mind
his disguise his game

gorgeous dream a
gorgeous treachery I
wonder about armor
trajectory consumed by
my own plans
hopes an obsessive
counting of one foot in
front of the other the
dark hides motive motion
reins in night birds owls
blackbirds who scour
the ground and sky
for mice and seeds and
the wolves and lizards I
know not to feed afraid
of what they will do what
I'll become in the night
with night's hold over
morning

the furies call for misery

no sleep open mouth the
furies call for misery they
call it a pipeline to God a
pipeline to hell they plant
seeds they plant fire they
are as trustworthy as you
are they say *own your
wanderlust and your lust
lust* it lives it dies lives

and dies they don't believe
life is sacred the
furies know *nothing* is
sacred they know the
stunning cold and lost of
anger of despair these
tools they carry
their radiance their silence
the air is full of furies their
dank and heat misery their
element seductive their
serious addictive play

orphan, light

once upon a beach and
upon a wave and
upon a cloudless sky a
cloudless intimacy a
cloudless laziness and
into that blasts
certainty and uncertainty
both occupying
hope at the same
time they wheel they
endorse they cajole like
the best and better
angels they
go an octave higher
than seagulls an octave
higher an octave after

an octave we can
play games all
we want the world
always patient even
as we destroy it what's
a given is how
we forget have
forgotten always
will how the world's
in our image it's ruin
our ruin an
undesired suicide we
do this to ourselves we
look in a mirror empty
gaze agony and awe
at all we stand to lose
the wild

flowers of evil

across the city the
jacaranda trees have
begun to bloom
begun their lavender purple
assault on the
eyes they are
lovely I am not the furies
continue their
call their siren their
song my lizard mind says
look at them the

jacaranda says *spring*
is not too far away this lizard
wants me over
the edge lizard the cliff
at the border of a country
where my body sits
in desperation gutter and the
lizard sleeps the sleep of
satisfaction

conditional

temptation seduction take
pleasure in the every day
of survival of letters and
words on the page a
found lost a sudden
sound dropping coins running
water a single bird a
note written last night in the
morning makes no
sense *my father says*
that's it that's all nothing
else it doesn't look
like my handwriting or
his or Katherine's so who
was here what *I* what
father what *said* as if
words to be *pegado* (fixed)
in place blue yellow white
ceramic tiles on a wall

so many consequences the
temptress *la seductora* dark-
eyed elusive and metaphor she
comes in the night she says
hold me hold no other she
wants me to want longer the
dreaming night

when my mind is not my ally

January has the
Wolf Moon in the
sky in its hunger its
claws and knives the
demons are out the
nights demonic they
pick their teeth with
the wolf's knives who
wants to risk that
except those
forgetters of risk so
in forgetting no
risk at all just learning
too late what the
moon has done what
the mind has done
someone laughs
somewhere cold immoral
cruel me it is
me the moon under
the sky be the

demon flee the demon
wonder when
freedom is freedom

The furies

> Kiss of your agony Thou gatherest,
> O Hand of Fire
> gatherest—
> —Hart Crane, *The Tunnel*

> You need the shadow of a child
> Like an avalanche
> —David Shapiro, *Spring*

> E io, che di mirare stava inteso,
> vidi genti fangose in quel pantano,
> ignude tutte, con sembiante offeso.
> —Dante, *Inferno*, Canto VII

1.

                Mexican landscape
mountains mountains mountains
great dark spreading and

    voice
    in my
    head of
    my head
            of too much
dust too much light and
sadness numbness
the world in

collision or collapse an
inability to even say
words my words any words of
disappoint confusion of
love reassurance
                they my furies

2.

come whenever they
want to come in
daylight dawn midday
the pursuit which isn't
pursuit because they
are always here pursuit as
present present as
pursuit
they with
talons sweet faces (illusion)
with poems song they
enter my body they
insect swarm they insect
invade they insect (sweetly)
here to help destroy
(the streets filled
with rainy season rivers
carrying leaves carrying
those voices which
will later fill the
rain which will
later fill the air

and the streets
grow more and
more like rivers I
don't remember ever
over decades this
much rain this
many ghosts these
many broken words rivers)
they
to
read my mind here
          invading
          here
          to

3.

          hold in
dystopian night
dreams nightmares
the new-found old
disease (their
sweet faces their
sweet songs songs
we sang marching
we memorized we down
by the river we who
would not be moved we
were always moved we
were always lost their
sweet nostalgia how to

tell these inhumans from
the others from the
angels the muses how
to know what was
howl what was body
a body ready ready
for sleep there is
where the beauty save
there is no beauty
there is no beauty there is the

    4.

despair)
                they live
off fear and love from
fear and fever how and
with you (me) your
(my) whole life in childhood
they seemed worse
fear even worse they are
than death to live through
that splitting the burning
trap suffocation something
even to the gods unbearable
and even to God how
it would be the end of
stories the end of
faith of hope the lifelines
erased life disappeared
the political disappeared the

children disappeared the
history of the world
the ghosts who
call them the memories
who call them
this is their power they

5.

like the ghosts at
the unmarked ruins the
buried all you see
a hill a tree piles of stones
or in the market where a
woman with herbs you
ask her a question she
says try these a
mix she makes she
shakes her head it's
the best she can do it's
all she can do she
(about to say something)
stops

   because there
    inside the dreams again
in the body what the body becomes
attacked and no alarm no
warning just the breaking open
of the earth the cracking open
a shell a thin young tree

a mighty old tree a body
like the earth the body falling
the trees falling falling buried
by everything becoming in
itself of itself the furies
there with their anger
their disease they are
born of night or blood drops to
water or air and earth
—anger   rage   revenge—
their bright eyes
dark glowing with

6.

                    the sun the
midday sun the
empty city you
think (I think)
ciudad de fantasmas
echo of steps no
voices there's bird-
song there's street dogs
in the park at
the newsstand no one
no one and no
newspaper no *diario*
to say the news
you already know the
furies swarm the
skies overhead they

settle in the trees
waiting
for what
for you to think
to feel so they
know without seeing
exactly where
you are

7.

the furies they
took our
heroes who
stood up who stood who
were beaten down
in peace in protest in
love they took
them we let them we
because we clueless
helpless ashamed we
had become
less than the
one who doesn't know
to inquire we
     fell
     we so
     afraid we had
     become
     of light of
     daylight of

how much must
fall before
the truth

8.

is this
what they
are for
you are
no hero
poet make
your peace
with age
make
your peace
with death

death
the world
death
the loved
death
your own

make it
peace
as if
there was
a choice

as if
in saying
no
there's
something else

9.

      it's knowledge they whisper
(soft) they know everything they
live with the truth the horrible
truth and the horrible
whispers and the horror that they
are come come to me to
places and bodies to mind and
hearts come to me where
they belong

sanity

what's left on the
roadside the tossed
refresco bottles wine
mezcal plastic
bags chicken and pork
bones thigh bone rib
bone everything connects
to the head the skeletal
wadded up toilet
paper old newspapers
a series of articles on

femicide and genocide a
series of articles *the vaccine
won't work the vaccine
won't cure the evil inside
us will out* tossed cans
beer beans an old pair
of jeans torn and
stained with grease one
shoe one *chancleta* (flip
flop) stomach agitating a
sign indicating a winding
curving road a winding
darkness so much
obscured no matter eyes
open eyes close a voice my
voice speaks up it says
sing it says *turn on some
music and sing* and as
loud as I can I do I do
into the air all alone

te estamos observando

> —sign on a Oaxaca street warning
> thieves to stay away

en la mitad de la noche the
middle of the night they are
watching me for what for
why *observando, mirando
oteando* against thieves all thieves
protecting their streets but

for those who sleep then what
in Puerto Rico they tell children
stories of *el coco de la noche*
who comes at night who
comes in dreams who steals
dreams and makes your dreams
his own *soñando en ti soñando*
en mi dreaming you dreaming
me he takes my dreams and
you are his and I what am
I *mirándome* you *mirándome*
you look but see only
el coco he rises above
the sheets he takes you in
his arms *te agarramos*
al infierno we catch you (me)
to inferno they'll throw me and
that leaves you with *el coco*
who laughs from the
other side of the womb other
side of the street the
world he holds you tight
while the neighbors watch
they watch the long
night waiting *te*
estamos observando

some history

we lived in
darkness

disease
a place of
disease
and fire the
earth opens up
the buildings come
down the people come
down villages
swallowed by rage
fear they disappear
into dust there's
dust everywhere it
seals the
disappearance
disappeared

home I take a
panuelo (bandana)
clean the
dust off my teeth my
face and look at
the mountains our
fields my
neighbor's sheep
and goats herded
by his children

on the walk today
on the
dirt roads called
highway a

boy had appeared
in blood he
seemed out of
nowhere a truck
had come by a
sudden scream the
truck was gone
and the boy from
a village hours
away he'd been
attacked beaten he
had no money he
had nothing
they'd thrown
him in the back
of the truck they'd
driven hours
and just here
dumped him
dusty ravine we stood
there myself some
farmers suddenly
emerged from
the woods and
gullies men women a
family came by in a
pickup stopped to
see this crying
beaten boy
maybe thirteen he
held out his arms

dust blood I
gave him some
water what else could
I do we watched
as he walked
into a field a woman
with a *machete*
went to him
she talked came
back our small
helpless group she
was shaking her head
she said something
about God he
walked in circles
he fell down and
we stood there
needing a doctor in
this place we
don't have one

tectonic

the *sismos* that
threaten always
threaten the pressure
comes from everywhere the
core the storms the
flooded earth the dry
earth and the voices of
days voices of memory

my father's face anger
love my father's face
and what the sky looked
like as if the birds
could nest there but
no nests in clouds no
cloud cities no
worlds this world holds
more than it should and
that weight that weight
more than it will bear
the rivers the
oceans the voice of my
father the voice of my
son that's how pressure
feels on the heart but talk
means less than what will
happen with the *sismo*
it will be a touch
on the cheek a blow to the
skull watch now how the
world opens watch now
all we love
devoured by the earth

the sins

the bear went
over the mountain and
the sun did and
the moon rose the

rain fell it was
a delicate moment but
we lacked the delicacy
to see it more correctly we
didn't notice the light we
didn't hear the
birds we didn't stop
even for a second so
filled with the
business of life
here is how
my soul becomes
a wreck a wrecking
ball resting place
for deception or deceived
ocultar and *esconder*
both mean to hide
but *ocultar* it's by
masking and *esconder*
putting someplace unseen
once someone told me
I can read you in your eyes
and closing them I asked
what color she said
I don't know and
I said *blue*
she said *you're a liar*
a liar I thought
I opened she looked
okay she said
you're not for now

down the drain

there's always an
argument the quiet
of the night vague
not well thought out
not planned there's
buzz of mosquitoes
the close air of the
bedroom so we
open the door for the
breeze

the argument is
heat and sympathy a
spell cast the
suspicion and invasion
of snakes and lizards
scorpions and the
prima donna stars
they ask for a prayer
to the Virgin or maybe
a prayer for no one
no one knows what
part of the world
would be good enough
for the long rest
and the long debates

because that's what's
always a fear we

would go on like this
forever never stopping
the argument never
the Virgin prayers
the scorpion's tail curls
the serpents and lizards
show glittering eyes
a brightness
now like the lamp light
in the room

legend

that skeleton in the
sky is a bunch of
clouds a trail of
firework smoke a
beauty who was found
to be quiet and in
the streets a cry from
the earth a cry destitute
what do we want
no one exactly sure
daily bread and maybe
something else a little
joy maybe some wood
for the cold night it
might be nice to
have a fire then
there are a few
rivers on that side of

the mountain nothing
really to fish for
some trout maybe
we pan fry it a
little bacon
impending thoughts
will come
thundering herds
or weather a great
flood of words but
what do we do with
all that meaning it's
a sad game that feels
a little like something
already known already
repeated one too
many times we know
life is like that when
it really happens the
repeated repeated
we know there's
nothing new
under the sun we
know to make it new
that's how legends
are made
repetition repetition
like her over there the
legend drawing cards
from the deck and she
reads them to us she's

unhappy of course
with what she sees
todays she's a
doomsayer a sayer
of the truth no one
wants to hear Cassandra
spoke as loudly as
she could she
wasn't burned at the
stake but she could
have been she was
someone to watch
standing there in
front of the crowds
divinely touched divinely
doomed our
legend shows us
a card she says
you're falling once
again and you're
once again lost and
it's once again ocean
and once again
silence blindness
she decides she'll
draw no more
cards and when we are
ready to leave we
ask what's the point
you were adrift she says
the world is adrift she

says you have
only the ocean there
where no one knows
the depth and the
other shore

nothing worth nothing (haiku)

full light is a
blessing deep
beneath the
sounds of day I've been
wandering around the
house wandering through
the streets as
someone who has
place and no
place aimless
and with purpose
I've been through
nowhere a few
times it sometimes
feels eternal one thing
after another
people walk dogs
a woman sells loose
chewing gum sells
cigarettes some clouds
rest in place until
the sun heats them away a
breeze a wind from

this park bench I
couldn't complain even
to look in the mirror

but what will they eat

that purple sky
glows north those
mountains the day's last
sunlight they
read a manifesto today
on the university radio
one written decades
ago acute language
precise clean

and
I feel I'm back in another life
not mine really it never was
but I feel what it felt like how
it made warriors out of ordinary
men and women in
fatigues *compañero compañera*
the whole world
witness to gunfire and explosions
to the storm silence
to re-rehearsed
words and lovemaking on beaches
in forests sand and earth earth
and sex we sweat
freedom where we

had been where we were
going vision after vision
until our now and now and it's
different

diseases cover the
cities the world the countryside where
a man on the side of the road
raises a bottle to me smiling
he's drunk cars roll by him
horns honking his bottle a salute
to the purple sky
twilight a revolution
song against our
dreams our dreams

in whose night we carried
water bottles and books we
read deep and to each other in the
nights surprise a conversation an
embrace by fire notebooks
in our pockets we wrote
poetry we wrote songs what

do we write now what do
we think now the nights down
nights always down the sky
uncaring unconcerned there's so much
left to do it will never get done the
curse is *that* truth *that* certainty no
matter how far on the roads

we made and traveled

sought path

too many there too
many and rising
sky or birds made
to clouds made to

birds a sign in
the street *enter*
a sign *leave* a
black cat across your

path a gray cat
sister tribune
trees dropping flowers
orange white petals as

large as your hand and
fragrant and still a
kind of nothing not
emptiness but

sin sentido no
meaning no feeling a
voice that comes out of
nowhere your own

how close could
this be *in your voice* to the

real the absolute
the one once sought and

now abandoned a
building or a city from
centuries ago now
collapsed ruins visible

no one dreamed this
moment no one desired
it what we see we only
half make the rest still

hidden waiting for us
or discovery desire
in the earth the
bird-filled sky

running

some winter road a
peak mountain a peak
exhalation of breath
someone says
I'm happy to wake
up today the moon in
the morning sky a
kettle steams a
beep beep of truck
backing up the air full
and sirens ambulance

fire trucks enticing voices
of alert a song to drive
someone mad even
tied to a streetlight
pole wretched hourglass
time has a way of
doing these things
unexpected a whole
day has passed but
it's still morning or the
day is over where'd
it go filament of
fishing line old light
bulbs in a box in the
closet useless too
useless even to throw
away

when all the words no longer mean

I'm not sure
what to do when
language deserts me the
emptiness and loneliness
that comes with that
I can gesture at a flower
and there's no name I
can think I point to
that bird in *that* tree or
over there towards the
mountains a town but

I can't tell you
which or what
maybe by language
and words I mean
names specifics like species
or genus geometry or geography
that thing for
making tea (kettle) that
thing for digging holes
(shovel) Gregorio shows
up sometimes and instead
of using the weed
whacker to cut *la maleza*
(the weeds) he uses the
machete I bought at the
hardware store actually I've
already bought two and while
I think they could
use sharpening he says
they're fine it's only
grass and weeds some
dead branches and
carrizo which is like bamboo
I spent part of the day
today clearing some
space in the drive that
was overgrown a quick
strike with the *machete* the
carrizo tall thin snaps
and falls we burn
it out in the field I

worry about that burning
but Gregorio
thinks it's best that
way at least easier no hauling
of branches and weeds
some of the *carrizo* we
use for repairs
to the fence and
some for blinds on the
patios Gregorio thinks
the ash is good for the soil
he's good at controlling the
fire so it doesn't spread I know
nothing about this but
it's okay my ignorance
because days and
days pass by I
might not understand a
single fact a single
sentence of anything I
hear or read it's
all the floating signs
and symbols
I look at books even
books I've written it's
a blank a blur I've heard
this is what depression
is like moving
through one's life in
dullness and fog I'd
love to think there's something

out there can bring back
understanding bring
back flavors bring
joy I don't know
maybe something
in medicine
will save me

resist

whatever the furies
invoke whatever
birds in the *flamboyan*
flame tree whatever truths
and lies of
the world mixed
together so the clear
and the opaque mirror
each other so
much light and so much
darkness then there's
nothing to do but
head to the
streets into the
masked crowd we walk
along as though a
river walk cloud-like
fog-like we become
invisible without
vision there are
flames to the

sky from out of our
hands we have moss
on our foreheads
leaden hands
with the rising sun
setting stars we check
hours we check count
down seconds we
become the dissipating
crowd dissipating anger
unrecognizable and
unrecognized the lined up
in rows resisting

baptisms

air earth fire water
nothing for the
last minute not
even the smallest
most minute of the
creatures winged that
rise out of the
earth it's the
spring of our
intentions spring
and renewal
spring and promise
there's comfort in the
desert the mountains
even on fire and

the country in a
drought because
we can we pray for
the rainy season
pray for rain we
see no clouds in any
direction nothing but
that old enemy friend
the sun

bye bye *tristeza*

the furies on the
wing on the beach
in the cab crowded
in trees on streets
of cities *pueblos*
road-side storm-side
crowded on trains on
boats on busses crowded
into rooms bedrooms
and into our beds
they stain the sheets
they shred the blankets
crowded into bars
cocktail hour dining
room dinner hour
crowded to twilight out
of daylight out of
paradise the unnamed
furies the faceless

furies crowded into
everywhere crowded
into the desperate
nowhere now into their
own dissolution own
discontent disaster the
furies reveal now
faces names
toothless and blind we
call them misery call
depression sadness fear we
watch them they
fly off slowly wounded
undone beaten defeated
in their leaving we
look around at a world
broken we lean in
ready to heal

fatigue

sometimes
late afternoon a
body in collapse
late afternoon sun
shadows across
the room it
feels sweet
on the couch
book at my side
my shoulders sink

my spine sinks my
neck and head my
hips my legs it's
all a great sinking
and sudden sleep

fifteen minutes
exquisite then
abrupt open eyes abstraction
thrashing where's that
book I was
reading the poems
of Nezahualcóyotl—
Nahuatl for fasting
coyote—the poet
warrior king

jump the night

for the arrival
of dawn the things
we might lose
today ivy jasmine
maracuyá, iniquity
and caves we

look for lights at
the ends of
tunnels we look for
a world less
cunning devilish

frightening it's in

gunshots it's in a
blade there's an
old print in my
memory St. Sebastian
and his bleeding we
all our sadness

resistance dream

one morning they
came furies they
came with

screech came with
scream their glee
they came ready

armed with
words stories
came armed I

made a place
for them at the table
place for them in my bed

whatever they
asked I gave tears blood
sperm when I gave

gratitude and refused
rage I saw them catch fire
saw burnt wings

the flames burned them
brighter brighter their
bodies not bodies they

burned into ash into
figures of ash their
wings beat ash nothing

left but ash and
unmoving angelic their
feathered wings

II. My father's voices
(*sueños*)

naming a clock on fire

—for Robin Mookerjee, in memory

your sly
smile is in the
next room
the next
sentence
not already
thought
not
already spoken

how about we
meet for
a drink
how about we
talk about poetry

how about it

how about how
the universe chooses
to space itself
stars from
stars planets
planets
the universal
junk
dusty and filling

out the
imbalances between
even the all
invisible

the work to
do the work
I'll do
you'll do
invisible and
tricky

so how
about we
meet for
a drink
we talk
about
all that

okay

okay

okay

okay

in this dream nothing happens

—for Ilhan Sami Çomak

no *pointless wars of the heart*
though Jupiter and Saturn
have been that close in the early
evening sky the waves
continue their rock and roll there's
memory voices faces
the past on its own arc and the
present arc a rolling curve

nothing in the
dream nothing but a
weaving music sometimes violin
and strings sometimes brass and
voice and those ocean
waves it may be just the
radio (music) it may
just be beach the
dream disappearing in the
dawn and with that the remaining
sleep

odyssey

Kenneth used to
say how Virgil Thomson
said *ballet is all*
about saying hello and

opera saying
goodbye the
long voyages long
train rides car bus
plane we park and
plan by books take
notes careful to
expect the unexpected
maybe people maybe
place a trout stream a
church or cathedral a
painting someplace out
of the way that in
seriousness the
guidebooks say no
one has ever seen

we might hold
hands along a riverwalk
we might decide to
sing a song we love
one of us starting the
other joins in or we
might be alone far
away the day of a
blizzard or earthquake
quinceañera fiesta or
sacred time saying
to someone walking
by *I am Nobody* the
Nobody exclaimed as

whispered affirmation
consciousness that
nothing really happens
until the voyage is
over and the return
we open the doors

expatriate

on the late night
internet radio
the announcer said
snow in Central Park right
now I could see it
see crystals see
lights and trees
their invisible ice coat
hear the hiss slick hiss
of tires on pavement
steam from manholes
steam from breath
some part of me
went cold with the cold
imagined snow on my
skin on my neck and it
was sad and a relief to
think this something I
won't want to feel again

surviving

some days yes
others less
hot sun setting moon
I asked some
neighbors if they
knew when the city
water would flow
we have to clean
out our *tinacos* clean
out the cistern it's the
end of the dry season
water in such
short supply so timing is
everything you want to
be careful to clean the
tinacos and cisterns
just when they're empty
and before the water
arrives it's not
the wondering of *what the
moon what the sun what
the days ahead will bring*
it's the balancing of
uncertainty and certainty
because the water
is anyone's guess

your other language

at the beginning of the carnival
at the entrance
a lingering at the switch
the halo shift
the shrinking cue for the
joker the wild card
with his *fleur de lis*
and his hands made
of wax

let's go down the road he says
where the trident points
the right way our disconnected
breath
the cold morning

nothing simply
yes-no
1-2-3
it isn't Marco (Polo)
or ringalevio
unannounced is unannounced
hello is hello
goodbye goodbye

but look what happens
when there's a pattern, a sequence
Mary looked at her son
(a miracle)

Mary looked at our son
(also)
it's not a problem of keeping
the stories straight
they're full of contradictions
they have to be
intentionally
to avoid any future problem

longing for
longing is just
one more veil dance
when something when
nothing

my grandfather in Mexico

after my grandfather died
my mother gave me a book he loved
Ancient Jewry in Mexico

he and my grandmother
came to Mexico on a tour
I remember the
photos he took they gave us
marionettes men dressed as
mariachis leather wine bags a
single large horn from a bull
my grandfather loved it they
kept coming back

Grandpa now I live here
ancient in modern or
modern in ancient
yesterday I went
and found the book

the ancient Jews
still roaming here in Oaxaca
they speak Hebrew and Zapotec
they speak to something sacred
languages
that survive me

the dead I've known

still live
I hear
their voices I
see their faces I
am with them
in places we've
never been
together climbing
over the Zapotec ruins
a small church
rises from a
village across the
valley back in Centro
I walk a park of
fountains and trees
people their dogs

children on bicycles
I sit in a cafe
coffee tea beer I
look in the ageless
eyes of the dead
they smile
it's good all
so good
times like these
death can't
destroy a reminder
too how awful
it will be
the day we're
forgotten

schwarze bupkes

whenever I cooked
black beans my
dad would smile
that Al Statman smile
it split his
face in two (always)
he'd say *what your aunts*
called schwarze bupkes
mis tias and their
Cuban Yiddish their
Cuban Jewish cooking
all it means is
black beans

but it made my dad
so happy to say
he'd laugh
schwarze bupkes
schwarze bupkes
schwarze bupkes

love and voices

shifting calendar shifting
weight what's there
is mountain tree shadow
maybe the truth across
the wide valley the
wide plain in yellows
fading green dust the
dry season the sharper
cool winter morning
sky up north snow
nothing like that here
maybe a little
morning haze that
burns off soon
enough in my

nightmare last night
like so many others
my father come
again silent forbidding
(again) my brothers too
we were all in that

dance trapped we
struggled alone we
struggled together my
father watched as if
not even there a
distant mesa
in my

nightmare my sleep my
bed I thrash about I
flail and the only thing
good is I finally
wake up and there is
Katherine holding my
hand me scared what are
these dreams so
lost I said *I'm sorry I
woke you too*

in the direction of the dream

the story loosely told the
bandito of evening
islands dotting the sky like
so many stars a glow of
desire of longing of
nostalgia elusive and
eluded heartbreak of
certainty the world goes
from one extreme to
another a song in

my head the whole walk
they ought to
name a drink after
you we could call it
sadness or
anticipate or
some day after tomorrow
there are no stories that
have to end badly that even
have to end at all the
streets flood with
people none alert to
what is happening none
aware they are there
in my seeing and the song
you can tell this by
the silence the lack of
confusion the day begins
as if twilight

this new nightmare

it went on too
long Katherine
said she was
leaving me she's
done there's nothing
I can do to
stop her she said
I'm tired of
you I don't even

want to talk she
said *I don't believe*
in you anymore
too long too much
I was out in the
streets they
were Brooklyn
streets Mexico
streets the streets
of Commack they
all became a
single street a single
street destroyed
they lead me
nowhere lead
no place there
was nothing at
the end of anything
until suddenly
a stop sign a
stop light red light
my father his
wedding band
removed when he
died now glinting on
his hand he said
I told you about
this I warned
you I told you
I warned now
what will you

do I now what I
you repeating sadly
angry he couldn't
stop himself

in my hour of darkness

today the disease worry
pandemic dengue zika
the last two diseases back
in the news along with
hepatitis though Katherine
did note there have been
fewer *zancudos* (mosquitos)
despite all
the rain and puddle
breeding grounds
while cleaning Alma found
two scorpions under the
big blue couch in our den
she crushed them with
her sneaker though she
said one had fought back
hard curling its tail
going right at the rubber
of her shoe she
claims Oaxaca scorpions
are pretty docile though I know
it depends the black
scorpions are like a
bee sting brown are a

little more serious and yellow
you might not make it to
the hospital alive Alma says
sometimes she's watching
television and they walk by
her arm on her couch *they
just want to live their lives* she
says her family will put the
ones they catch in jars
of alcohol which is good
for rubbing on aches and
pains the physical ones
not the ones of the heart
yesterday talking with
my dad again it wasn't
the same because yesterday was
Yizkor and it seemed like
maybe during *Yizkor* the rules
how the dead can't talk
about the afterlife don't
apply because when it
was time to say goodbye
I told him I thought he seemed
sad I expected no
real response but he
said he was okay
except lonely without
my mom who would
say to me later that afternoon
when I called her
how she wants to visit

Mexico but how to
do that with a wheelchair
on cobblestones and our houses
full of steps and stairs
he said I don't miss your
mother exactly because I
see her all the time but I
do miss being with her I
miss her in my arms

a voice asking

are you paying
attention attention to the
dreams are you
listening to your-
self to the
words in sleep
denying sleep so
hard to through
the fierceness of
not images not
imagining not metaphor but
my life and life
itself swinging at me
haymakers and sucker
punch body blows I
wake sweating bruised I
wake in wonder fearful
at what I'm
supposed to do

Katherine says
the people you see
in dreams are
extensions of yourself I
think they're not they
are alive they
live they breathe
down my neck my
hair rises my
skin freezes this is
not me against me these
are voices voices wanting
to be heard tell
me things I
don't know those are
new lands new
landscapes foreign
spectacular
speed traps country
and city disappearing
ruins before my
eyes under my tongue
in my throat
the unheard and the
victims the vanquished
camouflage of disorder
inheritance it's all in
the gathering dreams
nightly warning
struggle demons angels
making their

cases pleading
they talk
expiation atonement
fulfillment release they
argue for a
truce that says
someday sooner
than later they won't
come anymore

the far off

calls of
mountains south south-
west or west south-
east or
those calling birds
call flight call again or
nostalgia because
in some notes I saw
on a photo in a book
read
> *after 1931 there*
> *are no more*
> *family albums*

no albums no
family just
years and change death
arrives on time
suddenly there's nothing to

celebrate suddenly no one left
no family no friends
all living done

done
over
the calls from far away
the calls this morning
once drew me deeper into
other worlds worlds hidden
mystery with desire
I was more willing then
I wasn't afraid I
don't hate being less
than I was I
I get that
there's nothing to be
done still I'm
looking for the trick
to survive my own
clouded calm my
careful calm despair

failing faith

it all ends here
darkening horizon
darkening flowers the
order disorder
lullaby of birds and
machines

thrush
jay
sparrow

masquerade of
old loves old lovers
habits made
of daily life

and things said out loud
was he loved was he
remembered can you
see his face in
the mirror the clouds the
ocean the night

double vision
trees lake
of trees in the lake
the lake the sun

and the
fear these
stories will
disappear the
works a
part of
the long
trip that
goes away

dithyramb

silence (precision)
precedes the song it's
a dance a
mystery the field
full of drying corn
stalks the field full
of *muertos* flowers
orange and wild a
dance a wind a
dance of wind slow
waltzes an elegiac
calling to a
muse or a spirit or
maybe spirits living
in the trees the
corn and flowers
in the water a
dry well and
in memory in a
photograph seeing a
photo there's my mother
my father my grand-
mother grandfather and
uncles cousins aunts my
great-grandmother Sarah
as well she seems alone
in the photo standing
with her arms at her
sides eyes straight and

at the camera she
looks directly into the
camera the lens the
void measureless distance
made by becoming an
object being an
object an image a
thing like almost
everyone in the picture
she's gone she's
dead so my saying
their names in last night's
dream is a small spark
for their living
in sleep a spark of stone
on stone

arrival

a knock a knock on
the door a
turning of the tide an
unstitching of the
weave the wheel
slow boat to the
other side of the
world the
vagabond heading out
to silence and
port of call
rocks prehistoric

worn by endlessness
it becomes a safe place
to sit rest this moment
gets to feel
endless you
love the illusion you
love how you
float above
yourself you see you
looking out at this
harbor where you
suddenly remember
it is you were

lottery

take what you
need no family is
really cursed though
at times it can
feel that way if
one bad thing happens
right after the
other plagues lice
plagues boils plagues
sickness plagues
blood we get to
keep the first born
but the joke is only
so the plagues will
continue the joking

goes on and on
into the night the
mohel joke the
hat joke the grandma
jokes that sometimes
include a hat my
grandfather looks at
the cake on the
table and says he'll
have another small
slice he likes something
sweet before he
sleeps my
grandmother looks
disapprovingly my
father looks the
other way he always
calls my grandfather
his father-in-law *pop*
I don't remember
what he calls his
dad I call mine
dad I call my
father-in-law *Kenneth*
he calls me *Mark*
the world looks
symmetrical sometimes
and other times less so
lumpy blue-green spinning
my mother is
still alive so she's

not in this story

why can't you act like a father?

my most insane dream
in some time it had
airports and train
stations my brothers and
I were there someone
had died I don't know
who we were all
meeting up to travel together
to mourn like a spy Russell
approached me in
disguise wearing a wig
big glasses a woman's
hat he whispered *I*
heard you were looking
for a sinner then David
appeared his hair
long and he
wasn't gray he said *we*
have to get moving
we were at an
airport maybe Laguardia
then Grand
Central Station
they posted the names of
the trains but ours
wasn't there then
in the middle of it all

emerging like vapor like
steam as if from a locomotive
my father stood
I thought
smiling but it was a
frown he was angry angry
we had summoned
him but we hadn't or
I hadn't I was just
traveling I was on my
way to someplace else I
said *I don't even live
here anymore* New York
the United States not
my country not
me from the
vapor steam and choking
cloud hell-fire my brother
Stuart came too the
youngest one the one my
father so differently
loved Stuart had
his hands around my
father's neck we tried to
stop him tried to
tear his hands away Stuart
was crying and screaming
a voice from *duende* from
darkness spirit blessed
hated Stuart's hair was
alive around his head

serpents I thought
Stuart choking my father
suddenly then suddenly
he looked like
Jesse my son Jesse he
looked Jesse then Stuart
then Jesse then Stuart
again and again until a final
again it was Stuart just
Stuart rage coal eyes
coals and flames his face he
looked so much like my
father choking him choking
himself we couldn't
break his hold we all
choking my father none
of us could stop and I
had to wake up it was more
than I could take Stuart's
voice all that was left
except the look on his face
in the dream he'd learned
something he hadn't
done a terrible
terrible wrong

forgotten

a small pleasure is last
night's dream I
remember no

one came to
chastise me to
lecture me to
call me out on
multiple mistakes or
sins no one with
angry face or dark
flashing eyes no
pointing fingers call
for penance
retribution so last
night a reprieve last
night a rest or better
release I don't know no
matter the dream I
imagine it's nothing
I slept right through
the night and
woke up just at dawn
to a waking city
already at work

memorial

who wants to
go the
way of
all
       flesh and
not
       dictate how

to be
        remembered I
want to
be there to
write the
obituary to
speak at
whatever
        service
there is
I want to be
a
mourner to be
sad a little and
be one who
speaks
        tells a
story a
        joke
        who
raises a
toast in
my honor
comforted by
my presence and
by my absence
comforted
        I want to
        comfort
in love
        with love

anyone
who misses
me

imagined shadow

I think I
see you on the
street half a
block ahead of me
you're pointing at
the mountains or at
some blue green white
tile in the facade
or wall of an old
church you're talking
to an old woman on
the street selling
sliced fruit topped
with *tajin* (chili
salt powder) or
listening to that
street musician
(violin) wondering
can you request
a piece you know
will he know the
Bach *Partita* you
stop and look in a
store window the
way in life you liked

to suddenly stop to
comment to a
stranger walking
by *look at that*
you say *how's about
them apples* you ask
you turn suddenly
and from half a block
away I hear you
ask me *what do you
think* what do *I*
think I think I've
been thinking of
you of you I think
you are here in
southern Mexico
you're walking these
streets in
shadow and miracle
creating shadow and
sound you're walking
you're breathing
you really don't
do either anymore
and I think you'll
visit me here the rest
of my life

III. *Sigue la vida*/shut up

más alto, más bajo

whoa
a little boy said

the wave of the train
pitched him into his dad's arms
whoa
he smiled
no danger there
whoa I'm hungry
he said

and   *whoa*

playing horsey on the enigmatic beach
enigmatic majesty glory
of skyline and ribcage
lift-off tank engines

struggling for miles
in the direction of prairie or mountains
the other thing I imagine
spring rain fall colors
sitting with a hidden drink
in the ruins of
a city
where no one came to die and did anyway

memory calling memories
they taste good

they
to me
they are sometimes of
airplanes   trains   busses
crowded late nights
that hidden drink again
it's really hard
public vices
what I loved
about my privacy
was how nicely it fit
my life

it wears loosely now
it may as well not be there
let me tell you something
like *whoa*
like there's something I know
you don't already

shut up

let Ariadne do the
talking let Borges
do the talking let
Virgil let Sappho let
it be some other voice
other music other
part of the body an
arm the heart the
knees the waist let

them paint the Golden
Gate again or the
Statue of Liberty or let
it be Raphael his
Plato and Socrates gesturing
into the blue but what
did any of them
know of the Pacific
or lifelong discussions
of the Good or where the
north starts the south
starts or whose east is
east west west where
I live is the center of
my map sometimes
it is as if they were
only making everything up
as they went along
philosophy history aesthetics
looking for rules that
language is only going to
break into ruins all
civilization struggles for
parental approval
los danzantes at Monte Alban
are not dancers at all
but victims of torture you
can see you can feel the
pain and fear where did it
all lead because here
what we think about

most is water what
comes out of the pipes
you can't drink it is
snake venom it's hemlock
it's a bourbon on the
rocks where the ice
is a skull it leers at the
reader who drinks off the
drink throws the ice into the
fountain but not like
coin more the melting
circles of the
northern pole you can
go there on a boat though
the flyover is quicker even if
more painful for the earth
the earth which fights us
back hurricanes tornadoes
pandemics whole parts
of the planet in drought or
drowning what good is a
tree if it withers into
shadelessness and the shadows
of the dead have
no place to go no
heaven on earth what good
is a boat if forty days
is forever and there are
no nights and the ark
of the covenant is just
one broken promise if the

arc of history isn't
bending but breaking Han
Shan hides himself in
Cold Mountain but the
Kabbalists say mountain no
mountain on the sides of
so many corn grows on the
sides of so many the
chivos and *borregos* the
goats and sheep leap over
each other do the ailing
hills really skip like rams in
a bar so many decades ago
in the East Village Larry
said to me he was being
a Buddhist I thought he
was a poet he said
Buddhist he said if you were
to shoot me I wouldn't die
the idea here of illusion but
I thought then as now
why would I shoot my friend
who wants to die at all it
feels a crazy mess in
the giant orange flowers
outside my window this
morning hummingbirds
colibrí their beating
wings their beating hearts
if they slow down and stop
if we slow down and stop

well they die well we'll
die too

interrupted

to live
in beauty
and not
in interruption

interruption
a world
uninterrupted
seen

that tree
yellows   pinks
in
air
in wind a-
live

what's a thousand years

a night of sleep
what's a thousand clouds

a night of birds

what's a thousand rocks
view from the trees

birch beech
petaled black-eyed susans
purple cone flowers

what's a thousand trains
a thousand ships
I know the story
of her face
the launching
radiant ocean
of radiant beauty

how far underground
do the roots grow
the trains go
in yellow lighting

into that mountain
and a heart like mine, beating
goes to the center
we disappear laughing

that laughter
every night
owl laughing
bear laughing
coyote laughing

the disappearing heart
˙many questions

what this has to do with life

bird with golden wings
golden head golden
beak in the sky the
sun the world deep gold
polished in a morning filled
with light
              the whole street
breaks from quiet
voices a jumble mostly
murmur shouts street
sweeper and neighbors
I turn off
the bedside lamp I keep
on all night to keep
death at bay say
morning thanks I head
downstairs beginning too
still holding the thought
of that bird in flight of
sun and sky

what is the right thing

privileges and desire our
neighbors burn the
cut grass the cut
wood the air fills with
smoke that smokes
through the

trees it fills our lungs the
sky you can touch the
air fingers birds insects
they fly through it all then
away what they know
upwind bougainvillea down-
wind out of control that
flame

animales celestes

celestes celestial heavenly a
meditation on the
divine the Pope
has told us our dogs
can get to heaven and
why not what did they
ever do that was
so wrong no original sin
for them if you ask me there's
nothing original about sin
at all in fact often it
seems kind of boring an
oh that again
no matter how stupid or
painful like the banality
of evil or the banality
of horror you know what's
coming but what's to
be done Cannonball was
zen Apollo is exuberant

Katherine and I have started
to talk about the next dog
the one to help Apollo
into his old age the way
Apollo helped Cannonball
with his some friends have
said we should get a
street dog a stray adopt
though I also think there
was great fittingness that
Apollo is Cannonball's
great-great-nephew and why
wouldn't we continue that
line it's a thought we're a
year away from that decision
we want Apollo to be young
enough he'd really play and
train the puppy show the
puppy *siéntate* and *espera*
and run around with
a ball in his mouth playing
keep-away instead of
fetch tail high prancing a
little as he dodges the
chase a thought balloon
over his head *that's Apollo
the dog not the god* though
spelled almost the same

easing pain

wherever the light comes
from a window a door
wherever the
light a view of
                    a river
a river bend in a
river green over-
hang of trees the
quiet it's birds
wing flutter song call and
the water moving with
the sun now
the water
dappled sparkling quiet
                    moving
reflecting green and sky

hidden storm

in a memory hiding
from journey from
missing paths
trees from late
May mountain heat
over the mountains I
see clouds thickening
accumulating becoming a
crowd themselves
unsure if in mob

or celebration they will
be rain and thunder the
winds blow over
chairs blow the trees
sideways the jasmine and
bougainvillea petals all
over the air the ground
we knew this was
coming even though the
sun had been bright hot
we knew in the heat
and blue it would change
how the waiting earth
would catch it

the soul hears what the ears can't

on the wind on the
wind in the trees on
the wind in the trees
with the sun with
the wind then no
wind then no voice no
voice no clear hearing no
clear wonder no clear
surprise no surprise no
wind but daylight still
daylight all day it's
the morning the morning the
morning the sun the morning
turning afternoon turn to

clouds turning to wind
turn a truck far away a
truck bringing water
a truck collecting scrap
radiators and car batteries
mattress springs mattresses
a truck collecting useless
shelves useless grille work
useless and far away
still farther than the truck
a street vendor with
sweet *tamales* a motorcycle
delivering *tortillas* a quiet
a stillness a small voice
a dog stands in the
middle of the road stands
there and the truck stops
the motorcycle stops
the dog stands watching
the clouds defy the sun
watching as if no
movement the dog steps
slowly off the road there
the truck there the motor-
cycle all in movement
now and I'm not
moving I am the stranger we
the strangers did it a sky
full of birds clear copper

an earthly paradise

I think to myself
there is no such thing there's
no reason the two
together this
earth itself doesn't need
can't even support
too much divine and
why would paradise want the
broken science of
the earthly
of course a voice
in my head asks what I
know of reality I
look out the window at
this morning's shifting light
how the sun went from
blue to gray and now it's heavy
raining the tree at the
window all greens and
large orange flowers

the tradition of light

at my feet the dog Apollo
there's a dove in the
tree then the dove flown
to freedom it makes
fun of mine because
this dog will

not let me move it
took him too long to
find the exact position the
one that blocks me from
getting up now he's fallen
asleep soft breaths
slight quivering of his paws
he stretches a little
turns himself sighs
all more comfort for him
southern Mexico daydreams
spring always spring
here no matter the month
he's happy and I'm
trapped *ni modo* we say here
it's kind of like *tough luck*
or *nothing to do nothing*
to be done I could
make my move or
wait him out he
won't sleep forever there
are walks to be had
and bowls of food to eat
but that future isn't now
I turn my head the sun-
light in my eyes *ni modo*
ni modo ni modo

invierno (pre-pandemic) *Oaxaca*

inferno
cold center in Dante
but here nothing
like that it's a dry
breeze Christmas
season even as tonight
we light the first
Chanukah lights on

last night's walk through
Centro music around
corners the ubiquitous
chilenas with *tehuanas*
dancing the birth of
Christ *elote* vendors
grilled corn fruit *ponches*
once again the accordion
once again the small
child hand and begging

this morning the usual
December explosions
cohetes (rockets) celebrating
a month ending beginning
days that go years that
go one more walk through
the streets too the market
through the day through the
night the silence the

violence the wandering the
peace

      what time
passed is there anything
to notice
        yes/everything
            but
one would have to stop
one would have to stop
stop stop stop
and why bother when
motion is the point and
when change
and the same are
the same

time crazy

it was a
little strange how
memory put its
stamp on today
how in every moment
I sensed
the moment
has already happened that
I was living a moment I'd
already lived it was as
though there
was no now and no

future that whatever
words came out were
already there I
already knew what
I was going to
say what feeling I
walked down
Crespo down Tinoco y
Palacios thinking how I
remembered these broken
streets I'm on the wrecked
sidewalks the potholes
even though it was just
this time now still I already
knew I was seeing this
for the first time
and not what's already
known I reached the bottom
of the hill and before
arriving I'd already looked
at the sky already seen
those clouds which I
now see already
changing as I knew
they would already
disappearing as they
were going to the bus
about to pass me
has already gone the
smells in the air of
corn and meat no

longer there though I'm
standing ready this life
in the past the newspaper
I've read and still busy
anyway I'm going to
the market and my bag's
already full of food
fruit vegetables a chicken
tortillas it's almost like
a life lost from its own
routines its own my own
I've walked back up
the hill I've walked back in
the house I drank
cold *agua de jamaica*
hibiscus water
waiting to catch my
breath from the walk
waiting to feel in my
throat the cold already
of the water

Ocotlán de Morelos

sparrows on
the shoulders of saints
and archangels

bird songs
human prayer

here St. Jude
they're singing him
their singing

the saint
for the hopeless
the desperate
saint of the impossible

some curse him
their fate
others pray and
hear in prayer
birds

on the road

take the coastline and
mountains as serenity and
justice fierce battalion
of caracara and falcons
every step and twist and
turn it's a meeting of
the minds serpent on
my wrist the lizard they want
entry into paradise there
is no paradise there are
footprints body prints
platanos in the trees and
cocos frios at the
roads stands bottles of

mezcal silver glass glitter
in afternoon sunlight everyone
on the side of the
road half-naked in the
heat water steams off
them they wave at
passing cars at airplanes
overhead we all are
going somewhere fate
perdition paradise a
weave of time
of courage
and sky raptors it
takes hold with the
music on the radio
all the boys love Mary Ann
in the air with the windows
open and jasmine

mise en scene

yesterday twilight the
sky filled with
heavy clouds dark
covering the mountains
becoming themselves
mountains and the
thunder shook the
house the windows
rattled *sismo*-like
the radio weather

talked lightning
but it was somewhere
else I saw no streaks
across the sky no
bony rays illuminating
clouds there was no
rain when I
walked Apollo through
the city keeping one
eye a little fearful
at the seeming to
smolder sky but that
was the whole of it
intimations of great
drama intrigue and build-up
and no resolution no final
emotional physical build-
up no expiation by
midnight it was as
though there hadn't been
the twilight promise

inform yourself

if a break in
the action with a
conscious break with
consciousness that is
to say as if to
say follow the
story follow the

money follow the
jewelry follow the
time that's wasting
time always a-
wasting time which
is infinite time like
space how can we
waste time how
waste space with
so much infinity
with so much end-
lessness and possibility
so much loneliness so
much love and hope
and grief so much
the beauty of the
world from the
faucet to the
giraffe from the
line of the horizon
to the lines on
our faces the
growing hunger for
food hunger for
friendship a
warm body close in
bed to say good
night to say good
morning it's all
mortal all mortality what
a funny time to

be alive funny
time as if there
were a better time
as if we could
really say oh but
that's what I'd have
wanted that time
that time that's the
better time to be alive

I want to go down to the sea

a life by
water what it
offers its
sound
waves constant
constant a
measure of
time dimension it
and sky and
light a
mirror and
the earth

the blessed

are who they are not
even knowing themselves as
they walk or climb or
descend or stroll or

rocket or swim through
the world these streets
toward that park over
there the other
side of town sleeping
street dogs in the sun a
newspaper stand some
shoe-shines a fountain a
few vendors with steamed
grilled corn with nuts and
fruit chewing gum and
cigarettes candy a fountain
whose water spray glitters
sun skyward there is music
breeze an alert calm
it's all changing because
time passing but the blessed
are blessed not moving nor
stopped narrative and lyric
particle and wave

human spirit

I like to
walk this
city our city
see its age old
colonial streets
mountains
not too far off
sky and clouds

sun a
tropical mix of appear
disappear we're nearing the
mid-point end of the
dry season an uncertainty
here called
February crazy
febrero loco
the odd chance of
rains a sudden drenching
sometimes walking I
see nothing though
I like if when
in thought in
time I'll arrive some
place a plaza a cafe
a bookstore
this park today
the air light
with birds purple
jacaranda trees and some
palms shading
the paths on which
my thinking carries
me carries
the walk
suddenly it's
twilight first stars
the trees have changed
to laurels oaks pines
and the February dust

I decide to sit
for a moment
rest on a
bench in a
church
courtyard
that fills
with song
and prayer from
inside vespers
voices human
who call
against darkness

the trappings of light
design of the world
question of when falsehood
a lie and when truth we
place a coin in the mouths
of the dead I place a coin
in the hand of the woman
on the street who sits there
a half-eaten *tamal* next
to her she looks to be
eighty she could be sixty
what way to ask there's
no way she will not
be on the line for vaccines
the world's divisions
aren't usually subtle they
play out stupidly for all

to see I don't go looking
for God in too many
places *adivino* (I guess)
God is everywhere but
that woman is every day
in the same place herself all
in disarray thin a
small voice the
proposition is that the sentence
must say *something* I
don't know her sentence
the horizon glimmers
with the start and
end of day facing east
hope west night
I wonder what space to
claim what seat the air full of
sighs the echo of sighs
of uncertain
love uncertain lovers
who wait for morning
uneasy truce

a sense of humor

you tell
him the news of
his death has
been greatly
exaggerated or the
only emperor is

the emperor of ice
cream who has
no clothes he has
no horse no
beggars in that
kingdom no one
drowsing or entering
through a needle or
Leander-like the
Hellespont the rumor
mill there the one-armed
bandit the two-armed
lover sing
lover come back
the lover in rags the
lover rich with
stars with a crown
of thorns
crown the apostles
wear or the crowns of
mechanics and bus
drivers fruit sellers
the tortilla women
with *blandas* (soft) or
tlayudas (hard) it's all
or nothing and the
koan says to the
man with nothing
throw it away
the water falls into
the fountain a *peso*

for entry ten *pesos*
for luck

dos bueyes y una garza ganadera

two oxen and a cattle heron
clouds wrap the distance
and the mountains
of San Pablo Cuatro Venados
yellow and green purple grasses
an alfalfa field a *futbol* field
a well   a truck   a house
sky   cactus   fruit
no mysteries
the mama ox grazes
checks her calf
winged cattle heron walk
the mama's side

chicatanas

some mysteries have
to be that way
Alma asked me yesterday
if I was going to
the *casita* today
was I going to harvest
our *chicatanas*
giant ants from
whose toasted bodies
legs and heads removed

Alma makes a
sharp spicy salsa
the *chicatanas* only come out
once a year and every year
since we bought the
casita we've had them
they emerge before dawn
the ground wet it's either
on the 24th or 25th of
every June St. John's Day
I ask Alma
but how do you know
which day 24, 25 and she
smiles and says because
the morning after
the dawn fills with
small white butterflies

dawn

in alignment the
earth the chairs
the cafe the
tables the sky we
early risers in
quiet alone all
of us our own
worlds and in the
light that happens
with the suddenness
of dark

clinging to the present because the future

blue the leaves on
the trees the leaves
on the flowers the blue
earth the blue sky
blue mountains blue
ocean blue day blue
wind applause from
the wind applause the
day is coming day
arriving a fanfare
a parade and voices
voices rising up
not explosive quiet almost
a whisper maybe something
happening the
future sometimes
the expected or
mystery the
unknowns unimagineds
what's a world like where
nothing is predictable where
nothing is safe
on the beach the
children run in circles they
dig holes to the
middle of nowhere and
their parents drink beer
rum they laugh stray

dogs drag driftwood over-
head the *caracaras* (turkey
vultures) circle their
sky is blue their
earth is blue their cloudless
sky no rain

¿cuál es su tierra?

the dream life
exists the marine
life all life a tortoise
died on the beach
today black dark green
oval giant surrounded
by humans who wanted
to do *something* bring
it back into the waves
return it to the sea it
was bleeding from its
mouth we couldn't
move it it wouldn't move
no one could say how
old it was we
could see it was
battered yesterday and the
day before storms the
tide was coming in and
it couldn't swim
some of us stood there
longer watching while

the waves increased
pushed it up the beach
carried it out pushed
it back it was like this
a long time then one
last time the tide and
waves carried it out

Chachalaca Pálida

there's one in the
tree above the
pool gray brown
long tail feathers
dangling it
eats seeds
flowers turns
its head
toward the ocean as
if looking for
its own kind but
none Chivis says
there are fewer
these days people
caught so many
to eat *sabroso muy
sabroso* (delicious)
they don't lay
many eggs the
eggs *sabroso* too he
says he goes back

to cleaning the
pool I go back to
breakfast the *chachalaca*
squawks in the tree
eats gray brown
dangling feathers he
eyes the distance
solitude and ocean air

yesterday and tomorrow today

dry season and
dry season winds a
giant ancient
huaje tree fell across
a street no one hurt no
cars crashed but the
sudden fall meant
all southbound east traffic
backing up drivers
taking different
roads arriving late but
all the same
life takes me like
that every day I
think I'm going someplace
the park the bookstore the
casita and I end up
somewhere else the cafe
a plaza the library
yesterday Efraín and I

didn't talk translation
instead I looked at his
poems mounted on the
Henestrosa Library walls
with photos of rivers forests
unrecognizable women
and men we talked about
poetry and the future
certain of both without
knowing

you hiring?

the first thing
the weather's rotten
unexplained

the second thing
predicted future ghosts

how long to stay stay away
from the shadows
and the sun

stay out of the
ditch of loneliness
scandal

all exaggerated by
bodilessness
weightlessness

the words whose worlds we
suppress for all the best reasons:
no one tells our stories
no one gives us jobs

no one sings our songs
our love for sky and
night trees

no one goes free

the tallest trees
on the block
shade the block
from the sun

and at night
a forest darkness
despite the pavement
sirens
despite the ground light
which illuminates
the sky
makes the city clear

to the people
whose boats enter the harbor
whose airplanes descend
whose cars find their
ways to the bridges

different and different
and different and a
reminder of when
that city stopped
being yours

veneno

before we moved down here
Brooklyn Mexico before we
moved someone who had lived
here a while he's the painter brother

of a Brooklyn friend he said *Oaxaca's*
a very good place to come to die
which I don't think had much been in
our thinking uprooting to this city

of orange flowers of *calendas* (parades)
and *chilenas* (songs) of fireworks and
silence though it's true that death's
heads are everywhere that there are

celebrations of skeletons and skulls
mourning and grief seem as present
daily as mountains and sky as
present as dust the way Alma

noted to me of so much of it dust
in the house our windows and
doors always open but since we

are of dust as well why not

the air is full of life and poison the
water and maybe it's a great belief
in saints and souls great
faith in the worlds beyond this world

that death is not so feared this week
on the *zocalo* the giant laurel trees have
been uprooted the rainy season heavy
winds heavy rains of a rainy season tropical

depression it's all good for the farmers and
their crops and it means as well no
dry season drought this year there's
been some kind of rot in the tree roots

it started fifteen years ago I read
in the paper and now where once
it was cool and shade the sun's
harsh heat this early afternoon

blind

I was wondering this
morning about
omniscience about
knowing everything
as it happens before
it happens after
about hearing

every voice and all
the time and
knowing and acknowledging
about no difference
between morning and
day twilight and
night about every
season and every
ocean the facts and
fantasies of all the
living and all the
dead and no surprises
no doubts does this
mean no pleasure no
pain no falling in
or out of love no
silence or all silence no
loneliness or always
lonely or is there no
or but only and and
one and after the
other and and the
great accumulation that
isn't accumulating because
there is no adding
on there's just the
long string of eternity
which isn't long
at all because always
in an eternal
present of certainty

always all united in
omniscient consciousness I
wanted to put this
away I wanted to
stop this thinking but
I couldn't I couldn't
put away the fear abject
fear of what I could imagine
that was so impossible so
unimaginable and
believable that which
is beyond me that which
swims ahead so bright I
can't see no matter if I
keep staring into visionary
blindness that light

astillas

nothing too
desperate in the
air I can
make out the
sun the
cold morning I
wish I could
feel the poets
I know are
everywhere around
could hear
their poems could

hear my own the
spirit world is a
strange one it
gives a
little light sometimes
then the light
fades I'm left
with its
splinters left
to wonder with
what can't be
held too long

parachute, the practice of freedom

*I'm not scared
to die* Katherine
said she was
serious she said there
were worse things that
could happen so
surprised I went
out to the
mountains I
spent the rest of
a warm day
thinking of all
the better

IV. *Hechizo* (love poems)

besame

as if the last
time as if the
stars aligned their
singing constellations the
choral kiss and
embrace

        embrace
me as if the
meaning of rain and
the meaning of sleep the
meaning of order the
meaning of erasure
told stories

        tell
where in the world I'll
go after the
last words the last
hallelujah the amen
of being aligns
with a
walk up and down
the stairs
thirsty for a
glass of water

        how
the house empties

               how
alone among the
voices I'll
struggle my loss of
words and I'll
ask of you forgiveness
a ceremony
to replace resolve we
resolve we listening
beso

               that song

small lesson

Javier's daughter
sings along with
the radio playing
out to the cool and
cloudy Sunday
afternoon *lo que le
hiciste a mi
corazón* what you
did to my heart
she is too young
to have had her heart
broken at least in
the way of the
song there are
so many other

heart breaks
she could have had
she is nine
maybe ten our
hearts so easily
broken by the
world by politics
and dreaming there's
another song now
a *ranchera*
a different kind
of music and the
same broken love
she waves at me
the neighbor girl
in pink blouse and
blue jeans
leading her family's
sheep and goats
across the their field
and into ours
she's singing
along again her
high sweet voice a
little out of tune

the other side

first loves are
heavenly I would
want them over and

over again the
first days and
their breathlessness
is this me is this
you is this me the sense
of *unreal* looking
for all the right
words where does
all that go when we die
love and confusion
where is it all taken
somewhere occupying
space I don't
imagine recycled into
the world though
maybe it is that
way new bodies
new voices breathless
while we watch from the
other side silent
counsel

long days

the mind up to its
usual the summer sun
its usual too and rising
with my hands I'm
thinking now of
bodies touched in the
night and daylight bodies

some sometimes
forgotten I think
how the light those
days would enter
a room seemingly tentative
then certain the sun's
approach an imagined
conflict with night and
day locked into this as
if this were
the sum of all solar fortune
I was younger it was
always summer
most of the bed seeming
empty because there we
were lovers holding
tight I knew nothing
of the universe and conflicts
nothing of getting older
all I knew was the
moment the mystery how
wonderful and strange it was
to be in a bed with a
you so many *yous*
to feel like all my days
would be this

so close you can't see me

nor hear nor feel my
breath on your skin from

your telephone soon a
song who knows what
except I do I mean it's
Lagrimas negras
(black tears) calling
up the question of
tears I see nothing in
the sky save clouds I
hear a muffled silenced sound
maybe an airplane this
afternoon it will rain
it wasn't supposed to
nothing happens the
way it's supposed to
life full of lessons like that
even the heroes know as
blessed as their lives have
been it's only a matter of
time only the greatest
among them has no regrets
the rest walk along one
ocean after another one
road their shields hanging
at their sides useless
it comes less to fate
than to destiny they each
look at one another sure
they know each other's names
but no longer sure how
to say them a long time
since there was adjective

after adjective to remind the
world of what made them
unique I am sure you
know my name and I am
sure you know yours but
this afternoon we are
tongue-tied broken they
don't speak we don't
either

morning call

on an electric
guitar *sing the
blues sing the blues
sing the blues* we
all have certain
dreams are met
by certain fates who
come in threes
come in twos the
dreams the fates
become take on
form vision
conversations in deserts
the woods the
beach on a train this
happens again and
again visions and
faith visions and
faith St George and

the dragons St
Anthony Sheba who
does Eve meet who
Arjuna who Dante who
Nezahualcóyotl who the
earth the fates tighten
the threads
weave their webs a
complicated thing
being alive walking in
thought waking to
wanting to be
principled and good and
falling needlessly into an
unexpected ocean
over a cliff into
a well the feeling of
going down and doubt
it's where the guitar
begins the blues *sing the*
blues sing the blues
sing the blues the way
back up though
led to temptation
the equal desires of
resist give in

museum of the mind

rattling of pots and pans
viper in the closet a

broom there to sweep
away distinguished thought
distinguished praise
a man sits there in the
front row it's before I speak
he wears a linen suit looks
a little like my grandfather
or maybe one of his
brothers the Scherer men
you don't mess with them my
grandfather had a suit
like that he wore it once a
week my grandmother
washed it by hand she told
me how she loved
how he looked she
said this over the pots and
pans over the closet and
broom the vipers and
I had thought to say to her
but Grandma what about you
except how to ignore
her smile when
describing my grandfather
in his suit her vision of him
walking along some New York
City street or avenue it was
the 1920's *all the men and
women looking at him and
growing green* she'd say
my grandfather still so

young still trim *he was*
like a god she'd say
it made her that happy
pots and pans broom and
viper telling me about
my grandfather his
white linen glory

liberation army

—for my Mom

I know your story is
you loved with a
fierceness even God couldn't
undo even God
you tell that story you
like to tell of your song
how they tried
to tell you
you were
too young to love
you talk about
your rock there
in Central Park where
the two of you would go
as if that rock in
that city of cities
were yours and only
and of
all the years and all

the years and all
the years

your story is here
in these
southern Mexico mountains
a hymn a prayer sung
on high through me

now comes today
an insistence of
morning birds of
coming rains cicadas and
your loneliness too
that makes the story
fiercer and more
quiet still a
prayer always
a prayer sad and
sung always

Mexican songs

sound sometimes
holy sacred to me like
synagogue prayers
from when I was young
like the High Holy Days
and there'd be this
lifting this soaring this
sense of the presence

if not of God some
force beyond all forces
made from human voice

I hear *La llorona, Paloma
negra, Zandunga*
distant street accordion
distant radio distant
guitar and the soft
despair softness our condition
that's our turning to song
so that we in love
lost love
abandoned love
our tears
can say at night at
dawn we wing the
sun the tears (black)
a lost city a lost maybe the lost
forever

we in song long
for peace long for return we
long our spirits need
lifting how far fallen
we wonder at the life we
wanted so wanted
longed of and for we wonder
if not of then then maybe maybe
these days

sirena

out the door and
to go where
all thoughts are
bearable but with
so much movement
pain of knees hips
how far will I
walk this evening
with Apollo from
the Crespo home
to Xochimilco to
Jlatlaco to the
Zocalo then home
again Katherine
says *I want a boring
life* I think of
Odysseus reborn
wanting the same I
say okay
desire that is
opening my heart

manners

an anvil and
ordinary quiet things
basil sage municipal
parking lilacs primroses
spectators on the beach

flags flying jubilation
some great lovers
and their lovemaking
the he and she mixed
up coughing and
sighing their faces white
with pleasure one asks
why it happens like
this the other says
yo no sé no one says
anything else the
chicas and *chicos*
look back to the parade
to celebrate they can't
remember the last
time a good time and
as one a crowd they
look for private places
of multiple love nothing
too public that would
be bad manners which
matter when
defending civilization

listening

     and again
words around words
last day of March morning
our dirt roads marked
     by the fallow

fields the dry days
dry times
time of other work
repair replace all
time in time and
      still
roosters still goats
birds newly back from
further south
finches fly-catchers the
cicadas too back though
not yet their daily high-
pitched whine the
whine of call response
love seduction the once a year
courtship that tells
us yes here they are yes
the rains are coming
      across the
fields a neighbor has
been building a house
Gregorio says he'd heard
for the neighbor's
mother-in-law
      hammer
and music a song starting
with guitar

    take not your eyes
    take not
        your
            eyes

going home

the subtleties of
transcend or
destiny aren't
lost in arrangements
of flowers in the
afternoon *zumbido*
de las avispas
con pinta amarillo
(yellow jacket hum)
as they return to
their underground
hives

nor lost in
vision and a
ragged belief in
destined and
fatality in a
shrugging of
shoulders a
sense of doom
burden of
decision a

good idea
to take a
breath and
now to remember
what isn't real

what's beyond our
control and then

what it is
we can do
what allow we
could if we wanted
collapse into each
other's arms or
no
we could fall and
fall into arms find
our bed of
dreams the
bed of memory we
could renew vows
reclaim what was
never lost in
late buzzing afternoon
light

forever

frozen in
memory in time the
way a
photograph is frozen the
way a
recording is frozen the
way a
voice a face on

film in print filed
in a file in a drawer
in mind never-
                gone never-
                lost not
as long as I
                can breathe in this
cool morning in this
quiet house the
quiet houses of my life pre-
dawn so many
times the only one
moving through the darkness I
don't turn on
lights wanting to see the
rooms in morning shadow
the dawn as first
                light the
dawn its rosy fingered
evocation when I was
younger it was heroic now
it's a
practice
minutes and hours and
                days the
                days that
                spill that
                dissipate and
                disappear I
hear you say
no and no

> like the soft
> *dice no*
>> *no y no* of
> the *Los Panchos* song
> not a go away not a
> denial just a
> reminder it isn't love
> it isn't
>>> it's all image and
>>> *fugaz* (fleeting)
>>> the story memory
>>> presents and the
>>> present arming
>>> itself against the
>>> future that rains
>>> down onslaught
>>> of flood terror and
>>> beauty it never
>>> goes away the
>>> future even as
>>> I do go out now
>>> to the morning
>>> street out to its
>>> silence and
>>> endless air

desire moon

hearts along a
transversal moment to
cross the road to

cross constellations we
have placed unwitting
plans here and ignored
the future price and
its consequences if there's
no turning back from
pleasure then there's
no turning at all just
a stumbling through
bramble and thorns
bodies heavy and falling
forward in fog and
clouds of mind and
road we put on our
formal clothes the ones
we thought we might
never wear again I
want to look good in
my tuxedo wear a
blazing white *guayabera*
stark against black
and black satin

kissing

there's so much in
these photographs you
showed me yesterday we
are on a bench in Central
Park we are on a street
in Paris in San Francisco at

Christmas Oaxaca summer
it's forty or so years I
still feel that way we are
that young we are that
in love the years have done
so much loss grief we
had a child homes changed
worlds changed all the
poems all the paintings
dinners days a walk in
the park a walk on the beach
one walk after the other and
a life spent kissing walking
there's so much I can't
remember anymore even
the moments in the photos
themselves it's all so
different it's all
nothing all
something and the same

cross

the road or to
bear or your heart
on the
other side of the
mountain an overheard
conversation
nunca me amas
nunca me amabas

nunca nunca nunca
you never love me
you never loved me
never never never
the drum beats those
beating drums
words in flow in
flux in river
you see all the
patterns it's the
way you hear the
music from the
sky something
you'll remember
angelic voices
mockingbirds

clock watching

clock pot clock
waves clock phone
clock door clock
window clock night
clock mountain clock
moon clock again
what sense clock
abrazo clock cafe
clock bar clock
cab clock song
clock dance clock
sit clock street

clock again what
sense to make
sense to what
there the clock
there the pot
there the waves
there the night
clock hope vision
of you of
you of you
of you of
you of you

calling bells

sometimes there are
no words it's
just sound
unheard but there the
strangeness of what the
rest of the world
doesn't know the unheard
hard to explain I want
to ask *did you*
hear that too but
I worry what the
question would sound
like to the world
do you hear what I hear
sometimes it's almost
music a softness of

bells in the wind or its
the sounds of the
wind in the curtains
as a beloved enters
a room

consequence

there was a name to
the story in
the breach of night the
frontier breached the
mountains the
lifeline line in
the palm of your hand it
led to the eyes enchanted
it led to a smile your
smile the extended hand the
hand in hand hands
in hands then lifted to the
sky again as in I surrender
as in never surrender as
in I breathe I
breathe longer than the
forces in the world against me

for what it's worth
hold your body against
me hold me tightly with the
I love you that means love
means *I will let you go* and

never never never I
will never let you go

fiesta mortal

one kiss could
take hold of the
soul could send
us spinning off
the cliffs the masks
disguises we carry
on our bodies
tattooed with
equal signs and
parentheses hammered
silver copper we
own the world
because of love
because illusion
small beds of the
past boats on the
rise the kiss
changes winter a
fall and embrace of
knowledge eyes
that light up when
you enter the
room a boomerang
so many things
we never thought
and here they

are figures in
columns addition
subtraction I count
syllables sometimes
other times words I
listen for rhymes
at the end of the
day and how
love with love is
lined up

for the good times

a switch in
objectives the future
become accusatory fate
the present a refuge a
body standing guard
alongside and alone the
moment and then
the flood of questions
all predicated by
dream one and
belief two by
grieving three and
mourning four we'll
raise a cup to memory
we'll raise a cup to
love drinking down
something warm something
bittersweet more than

remembrance less than
completion by
daylight and moonlight we'll
say the same words how
these were the days how
though they're gone
we assemble now
assemble them
we reckon souvenirs

from the map

the looseness of
history and geography
meaning orbits
inside orbits unwed
to space to
clouds cloudiness
invisible hands or
something else the
hand tracing on a
rock a shoreline
small towns a
single city whose
citizens once were
from the small and smaller
places of no town
at all they wander
the streets someone's
demographic someone's
lovers they gather

at the city square in
silence not to be
counted named
traced maybe to be
seen not from far-off
you can touch the skin you
can smell it if you
hear them breathing no
words they refuse your
language your map

holy verses

from one room to
another or one
stanza to another or
one flame one
angel one idea of
prayer or saint or
the ringing telephone
singing telephone it
sings *sin ti* (without
you) or *son de la loma*
(those from the hills) or
canción Mixteca
(Mixteca song) it
doesn't really
matter it's only
words it's only
visions it's only a
sacred moment not

of time nor of
distance nor of
longing nor desire
it's not anything to
name to speak of
or question it's
in your pocket
in the heavens or
firmament you
don't breathe or
touch there's no breath
nothing solid maybe
you think *stop the*
presses this is big

canción

we could
drive the
highway
to Chiapas
drive the
radio on

we'd see
country towns
we'd talk past
and future
the present it's
always in

those miles
still ahead
and those
miles miles
behind

after the trees

which do not
live forever though
growing up I
believed they did
the way mountains
were forever
the way lightning
is forever the way
the plants the
way the ocean the
disappearing clouds
the way every dawn
because in memory
it's like that
what's the point
of memory if it is
not forever what's
the point of thought
of writing the
point of the poem
because after the trees
then what after
loving having loved

have been loved what's
the point if we
can't point at the
world say what
is and live with
that we are
right to believe
right to point right
to continue

revolution in the air

that couple on the
park bench my age maybe
older they're kissing and
holding hands and
quietly talking laughing
they look at each
other with the look of
lovers who have been
lovers for years the familiar
intensity of eyes to eyes to
eyes to eyes an ease with
which they lean into each
other their bodies easily
shift she reclines against
him he strokes her hair she
examines his hand in hers
holds it up against the
sky the whole world
passes around them the

whole park full of children of
dogs and walkers and runners
other couples on other
benches other lovers and
love's embrace the air is
clear this evening the sky
outline of giant trees of and
fountains

sometimes on the other side of the world

the soul and a sound of
pleasure and indifference hearts
claiming space an occupation
of integrity consequence of
one loved in the center
of the room an adoration to which I
affix ribbons affix hopes unencumbered
and maybe rain maybe sun I
walk a long walk deep in
thought buried it isn't the weight of
meaning as the problem more the
case for solemnity not a case
of gender on the sleeve skin isn't
soluble it won't divide it won't
add up I could put a razor to
the best intentions that would
leave a flock of birds
heading south and south-east
toward the sun the tropical

storms that evolve into hurricanes
tornadoes prisoners taken
along the way homes ruined and
the lives of someone's loved
someone's desire that when the
time comes the lines aren't
crossed the limits delimited
to see who cares it's a phone call
far away almost a dream to do
that look into your eyes
realize how little I know of
what you know and
how you understand

mls (heart) klk

there's a wearing
into revelation
stone trees seashells
mountains forests shoreline
cities highways
initials carved in a
tree no longer there
but whoever
carved them
when I was one
carving
we all think
they're there
memory memorializes
one kind of certainty

and holds its own
uncanny weight

hechizo

> *Lleva en el cuerpo la casa en ruinas.*
> *Abre la tierra,*
> *siembra algo que nazca no muerto.*
> —Marianna Stephania

1.

the image in itself the
image longing the I
love you and far away
I see your photo
I

                cannot see

                  you

                  you

don't   res-

pond   you

    in your distance in your
    difference you say I've
    never thought of you you
    say this isn't how I
    think you ask me
    what God I believe in you
    tell me some kind of
    story your own story your
    own God it isn't my God your
    story your words crush it's

my chest

I take

these words

one word written over
another you
would try to you would say

¡*ay!*

what would that close

what
will you

open will you

turn to me

2.

I have an idea to

put

magic in the

fire
make
some-
thing

more

than fire this
will take time for it's cue
from the gods

(there are still gods?
(there were are?
there is that

within me
which shall
tire Torture and
Time, and
breathe

magic   magic   curse

when I
expire; Something
unearthly

then the past
haunts the future the
the way the past haunts
me

3.

wind rose

      rosa de los vientos
      rose of the winds a
      map of the winds

the compass where
  does magic do its magic
    the winds
      have suddenly
        come up do you
          know how hard
            it is to

                    conjure
                        lightning
                            have you
                                ever been
                                    struck
                                        wizard?

                                            (who is the wizard
                                            (who is the wizard

        I
                dumbstruck if I
        look in your eyes I go
        down I go
                who knows
                        have you
                                learned I am
                                    helpless?

    4.

my mother says she is a witch
my Uncle Jackie was the wizard
I learned the hard way
do not mess with my family magic

    5.

magic older
than Hecuba older
than that witch that priest that older
tree it's a *pochote* tree it divides

earth from sky those older branches that
older river we are at the river we
are at the river older older and
older the fire

far-
gone the
world the ancient what is
the word I want to use to say *before*
there was a language before there
was breath before there was chaos and
order before there was the day or the
night you would walk around words
of careless inequality have
you heard the story of the wise
man he was an old wise man
he was our wisest wise man he
sold himself out to some magic
it wasn't temptation it wasn't
greed it wasn't desire he thought
it is an art form it is an art form I
can become the
  fallen in love I can
  rescue the
  fallen in love he was
  fallen into the
  wisdom of
    no
      and

6.

your word is an ancient word
your youth is an ancient world
your God is not mine but mine is
older mine will not refuse your God a
thing

7.

the wind comes
from all
directions the wind

fierce it is
fierce it is
going to blow the
house down it is
going to blow worlds
apart we have no
recourse but to
jump into the
dream not the
mirror the mind
wants mirror it
always wants mirror but
this shape across the
table this shape across
the dark night horizon makes
magic it possesses will
give you your sleep give

me mine it will put us
there it put us together
Something unearthly who
will wake up well
you asked the question
you decided you decide

Notes

The majority of the poems included in *Hechizo* were written after the poems published in my poetry collection *Exile Home* (Lavender Ink, 2019). In many ways, the poems of *Hechizo* stand as a companion to *Exile Home*, as a counter-balance and a counter-weight. I wrote *Exile Home* in the years that preceded and proceeded our move to Mexico and that book is full of the strangeness and joy, the exhilaration and inspiring confusion of leaving my own physical, emotional, intellectual, spiritual, and artistic world and of continuing so much of that old life while simultaneously beginning a new one. *Exile Home* barely touches on the global acceptance and even embrace of anti-democratic authoritarianism, nationalism and jingoism, as exemplified by the election in 2016 in the United States of Donald Trump, nor on the rise of ever widening poverty gaps, human rights violations in particular around race, class, and gender, and of continued environmental degradation; it also doesn't represent some of the other more personal difficulties and challenges with which I continued to live after leaving the United States for a life which despite those problems has given me greater peace.

In *Hechizo* I include some of those missing parts. I don't think *Hechizo* negates *Exile Home*. Far from it. I mean this book to include that strangeness, that joy, that exhilaration and inspiring confusion, as well as the darkness and inspiring certainty. *Hechizo* even aims, because of adversity, for the triumphal. So mostly *Hechizo* is really out there as an expansion and deepening of the story.

Title: *Hechizo*—a spell, one that can be used for good or evil purposes.

The Furies, in Greek mythology, were female deities of revenge. In *Hechizo* they gain their power and forms via some of my current and ongoing struggles: aging, alcoholism, deception, depression, faith, family, fatherhood, grief, illness, loss, pandemic, as well as my attempts to make sense of some of the 21st century's political, social, and environmental dangers.

Duende—a darkness and richness of feeling that is beyond language, a kind of inhabiting of the self by a creative and creating other that takes one above and to the highest most sublime connections we might make with the world. *Duende* can be a demonic, possessive force and it can be a liberating one as well. The presence of *duende* is an essential part of my struggle with the Furies.

when my mind is not my ally—Wolf Moon—moons have been given names by many different cultures—The *Farmers Almanac* is a good resource for these, as is *Shaking the Pumpkin: Traditional Poetry of the Indian North Americas* (Station Hill, 2014, 3rd edition), compiled by Jerome Rothenberg, one of my favorite anthologies of this kind.

the furies—E io, etc)—And I, there to look intensely, saw muddy people in that swamp, naked, enraged.

tectonic—sismos—the state of Oaxaca, where I live, like many parts of Mexico, is subject to constant earthquakes. It's located on three huge tectonic plates, North American, Cocos, and Pacific. Most of the quakes are minor in nature rarely above 4 on the Richter scale, but every few years, it seems, we get one over 7.

My father's voices—Albert Statman—1933-2018, my father.

naming a clock on fire—Robin Mookerjee —1962-2016, poet and scholar, a colleague and good friend of mine for many years at Eugene Lang College, The New School for the Liberal Arts; his death was one of several catalyzing events that led to the move from Brooklyn to Mexico.

in this dream nothing happens—Ilhan Sami Çomak—born 1973, a Kurdish poet from Turkey who has been imprisoned since 1994 to a life sentence for membership in a banned political party.

odyssey—Kenneth Koch 1925-2002, American poet, my professor, father-in-law, and friend; Virgil Thomson (1896-1989), American composer.

The *quinceañera* for a female teenager's 15th birthday is, in Mexico and throughout Latin America, a big event, often celebrated with a huge party. that can include formal dress, dancing, live music, and a lot of food and drink. In earlier times, it signified the celebrant's transition from childhood to adulthood.

surviving—a *tinaco* is a giant water tank, made of either a very hard plastic or concrete that sits on the roof of most homes in southern Mexico, often refilled either from a city or community water supply or via water delivery by trucks. Usually those water deliveries are piped into a below-ground cistern or directly to the *tinaco* if there is no cistern. The water is not for drinking without an additional purification system. Most homes have drinking water delivered separately in large plastic garrafones. Water, or the lack of it, is probably one of the more serious problems facing Mexico in the 21st Century.

in the direction of the dream—they ought to name a drink after you, from the song by John Prine (1946-2020), *Yes I Guess They Ought to Name a Drink After You..*

this new nightmare—Commack is the town on Long Island, NY where I lived growing up from 1965-1976.

in my hour of darkness from the song *In My Hour of Darknbess* by Gram Parsons (1946-1973); *Yizkor* is the traditional prayer service for the dead during Yom Kippur.

lottery—in Judaism the *mohel* performs the ritual circumcision on all males the week after their birth.

Sigue la vida—follow life

Más alto, etc—Higher, lower

shut up—Los danzantes—a section of wall found at the ruin of Monte Alban in Oaxaca state. Although it is made up of nude figures who appear to be dancing in fact it is more likely the carved figures are captured warriors or shamans from another city being tortured; Larry Fagin (1937-2017), American poet and friend.

human spirit—There's a phrase here, *febrero loco marzo un poco*—February crazy, March a little. It refers to the weather, how in February, moving towards the end of the dry season, we might suddenly get a lot of rain, or it might get very cold or very hot suddenly. And March might do the same, but less so. Since the rainy season really won't begin until April, the crazy weather is shrugged off. And it can be extended during February and March to explain almost anything that seems slightly different or other than expected.

cuál es su tierra? what is your land; this poem is an example of the poem doing one thing and life another. I'd been working on this poem after the ocean had carried the tortoise out and liked the way it was going. Then I looked up and saw that the tide had again carried the tortoise up and back to shore. There were about two dozen *caracaras* (turkey vultures) circling overhead in the air and then suddenly, as a group, they swooped down. For the rest of the afternoon and evening they ate and the next day there was just skeleton and shell and that the ocean soon took away.

Chachalaca pálida is a large bird that can be pretty hard to spot, both because it has become over-hunted in southern Mexico and because it is quite good at remaining out of sight.

yesterday and tomorrow today—huaje tree—The indigenous tree from which the name Oaxaca comes. The tree produces a pod with seeds that are edible and high in protein; Efraín Velasco Sosa (born 1977)—a leading Oaxaca poet and friend.

besame—kiss me

so close you can't see me—in the myth of Er. Odysseus, is content to be reborn with the life of a quiet citizen, rather than choose to again be a hero.

holy verses—the Mixtec are an indigenous people located in

Oaxaca as well as Puebla and parts of Guerrero.

hechizo—Lleva en el cuerpo, etc—from Marianna's poem, *Hechizo*, Carry in your body the house in ruins/Open the earth,/plant something not born dead; *There is that within me*, etc *from* Canto IV of *Childe Harold's Pilgramage* by Byron, this line is also on the statue of Byron in the Villa Borghese in Rome.

Acknowledgements

There are a lot of people to thank for their contributions to the making of *Hechizo*. First, my readers, an incredible collection of poets: Joseph Lease, Marshall Malin, Pablo Medina, Efraín Velasco, and John Yamrus. Their critiques, advice, and arguments helped make this book the one I want it to be.

I'm grateful, too, to another set of poets I admire greatly: Michael Anania, Joanna Fuhrman, and John Koethe. Along with Efraín, they have not only provided blurbs, they have offered the kind of encouragement that, even with *Hechizo* being my 11th book, I find helpful, nourishing, and necessary.

A lot of my close friends in the poetry world have used the time of Covid to reach out to other friends in the poetry community, to publish their poems, to give readings. I did a few online readings, but found that the work for this book required a different kind of focus, a kind of isolation, as my understanding of the text as a whole developed. So I didn't find myself in a position to even think about publishing individual poems. With that thought in mind, I want to thank deeply Paul Hoover, who published *shut up* in *New American Writing*.

In addition, I was quite honored and proud that I was asked to contribute to the *Free the Poet: Ilhan Çomak* page. *in this dream nothing happens* was published there and translated into Turkish.

No book I've ever written has not included Katherine Koch, painter, writer, best friend, wife of 39 years. There's a lot of difficulty written into *Hechizo*. But the final vision of the book is the vision in life. Rich, complex, and full of love.

Finally, a tip of my many hats to my good friend and publisher, the marvelous poet Bill Lavender. This is our 6th book together. His generosity, and commitment to my commitment, it's hard to put into words what that means. In a world increasingly and more awfully transactional, his support, not only for my poetry but the poetry of so many others, has become, most unfortunately, rare. It's a terrible thing because this world needs more, not fewer, Bill Lavenders.

About the Author

Mark Statman has written eleven books. Among them are the poetry collections *Exile Home* (Lavender Ink, 2019), *That Train Again.* (Lavender Ink, 2015), *A Map of the Winds* (Lavender Ink, 2013) and *Tourist at a Miracle* (Hanging Loose, 2010). His translations include *Never Made in America: Selected Poetry of Martín Barea Mattos* (Diálogos,  2017), *Black Tulips: The Selected Poems of José María Hinojosa* (University of New Orleans Press, 2012), and, with Pablo Medina, a translation of Federico García Lorca's *Poet in New York* (Grove 2008). Statman's poetry, essays, and translations have appeared in twenty-one anthologies, as well as such publications as *New American Writing, Tin House, Tupelo Quarterly, Hanging Loose, Ping Pong, Xavier Review*, and *American Poetry Review.* A recipient of awards from the NEA and the National Writers Project, he is Emeritus Professor of Literary Studies at Eugene Lang College of Liberal Arts, The New School, and lives in San Pedro Ixtlahuaca and Oaxaca de Juárez, MX.

Made in the USA
Monee, IL
07 July 2026